Piano | Vocal | Guitar

2ND EDITION

ALL-TIME
Christmas
FAVORITES

D1204324

ISBN 0-7935-3886-6

HAL•LEONARD®
CORPORATION

7777 W. BLUEMOUND RD. P.O. BOX 13819 MILWAUKEE, WI 53213

Visit Hal Leonard Online at
www.halleonard.com

BLUE CHRISTMAS

Words and Music by BILLY HAYES
and JAY JOHNSON

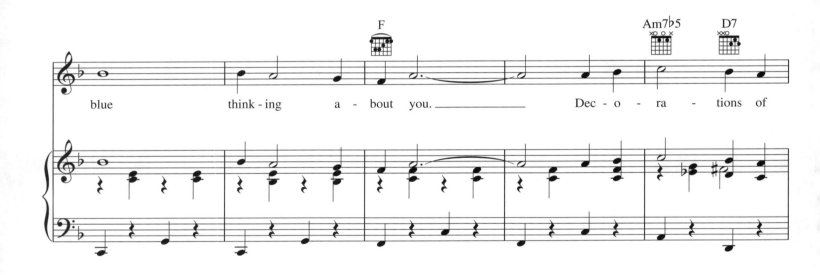

THE CHIPMUNK SONG

Words and Music by
ROSS BAGDASARIAN

Happily

Christ - mas, Christ - mas, time is near, time for

toys and time for cheer. We've been

good but we can't last, hur - ry Christ - mas,

CHRISTMAS IS

Lyrics by SPENCE MAXWELL
Music by PERCY FAITH

THE CHRISTMAS SONG
(Chestnuts Roasting on an Open Fire)

Music and Lyric by MEL TORME
and ROBERT WELLS

THE CHRISTMAS WALTZ

Words by SAMMY CAHN
Music by JULE STYNE

Frost-ed win-dow-panes, can-dles gleam-ing in-side, Paint-ed can-dy canes on the tree;

San-ta's on his way, he's filled his

DO YOU HEAR WHAT I HEAR

Words and Music by NOEL REGNEY
and GLORIA SHAYNE

FROSTY THE SNOW MAN

Words and Music by STEVE NELSON
and JACK ROLLINS

A HOLLY JOLLY CHRISTMAS

Music and Lyrics by
JOHNNY MARKS

HERE COMES SANTA CLAUS
(Right Down Santa Claus Lane)

Words and Music by GENE AUTRY
and OAKLEY HALDEMAN

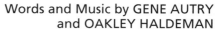

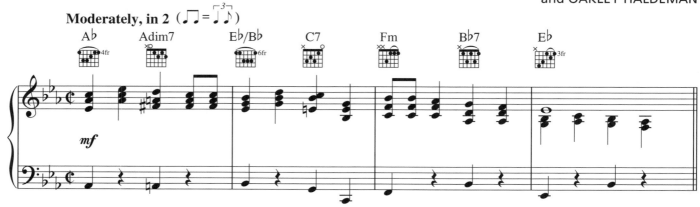

Here comes San - ta Claus! Here comes San - ta Claus! Right down San - ta Claus Lane!

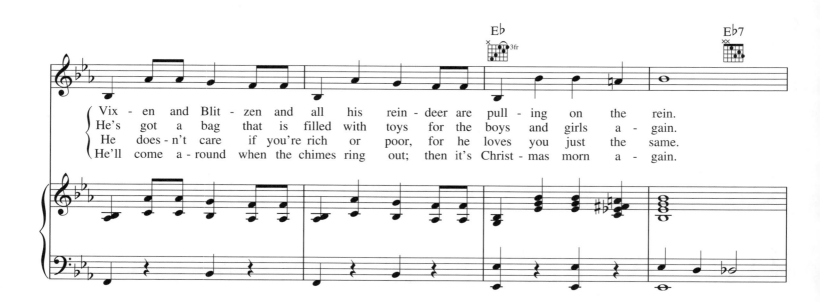

Vix - en and Blitz - en and all his rein - deer are pull - ing on the rein.

He's got a bag that is filled with toys for the boys and girls a - gain.

He does - n't care if you're rich or poor, for he loves you just the same.

He'll come a - round when the chimes ring out; then it's Christ - mas morn a - gain.

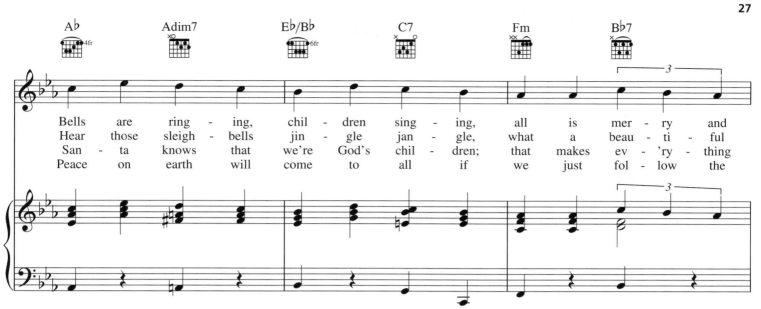

Bells are ring - ing, chil - dren sing - ing, all is mer - ry and
Hear those sleigh - bells jin - gle jan - gle, what a beau - ti - ful
San - ta knows that we're God's chil - dren; that makes ev - 'ry - thing
Peace on earth that will come to all if we just fol - low the

bright.
sight. }
right. }
light.

Hang your stock - ings and say your pray'rs,
Jump in bed, cov - er up your head,
Fill your hearts with a Christ - mas cheer, } 'cause
Let's give thanks to the Lord a - bove, }

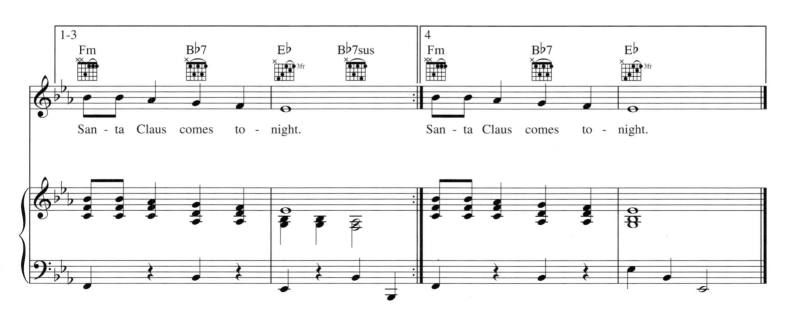

1-3
San - ta Claus comes to - night.

4
San - ta Claus comes to - night.

I HEARD THE BELLS ON CHRISTMAS DAY

Words by HENRY WADSWORTH LONGFELLOW
Adapted by JOHNNY MARKS
Music by JOHNNY MARKS

Moderately slow

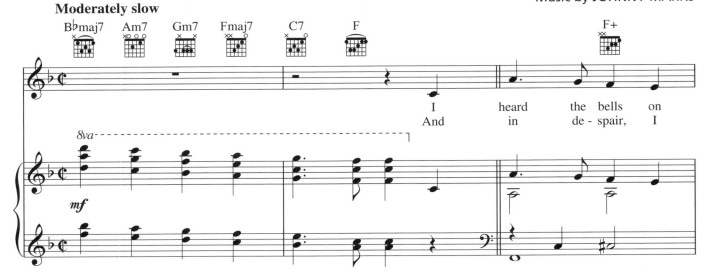

I
And

heard the bells on
in de-spair, I

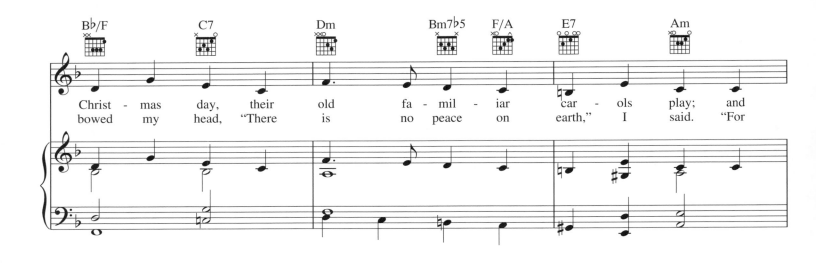

Christ-mas day, their old fa-mil-iar car-ols play; and
bowed my head, "There is no peace on earth," I said. "For

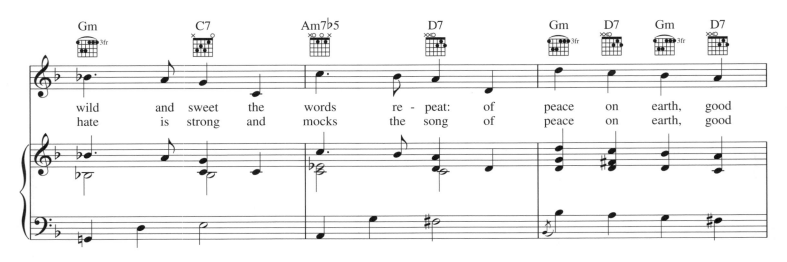

wild and sweet the words re-peat: of peace on earth, good
hate is strong and words mocks the song of peace on earth, good

I SAW MOMMY KISSING SANTA CLAUS

Words and Music by
TOMMIE CONNOR

creep down the stairs to have a peep; she thought that I was tucked up in my bed-room fast a-sleep. Then I saw Mom-my tick-le San - ta Claus, un - der - neath his

I'LL BE HOME FOR CHRISTMAS

Words and Music by KIM GANNON
and WALTER KENT

Moderately slow

I'm dream-ing to-night of a place I love, __ e-ven more than I u-sual-ly do. And al-though I know it's a long road back, __ I prom-ise you

LET IT SNOW! LET IT SNOW! LET IT SNOW!

Words by SAMMY CAHN
Music by JULE STYNE

Oh, the weath-er out-side is fright-ful, but the fire is so de-light-ful, and since we've no place to go, let it snow! let it snow! let it snow!

It does-n't show signs of stop-ping, and I fi-re is slow-ly dy-ing and, my

JINGLE-BELL ROCK

Words and Music by JOE BEAL
and JIM BOOTHE

40

MERRY CHRISTMAS, DARLING

Words and Music by RICHARD CARPENTER
and FRANK POOLER

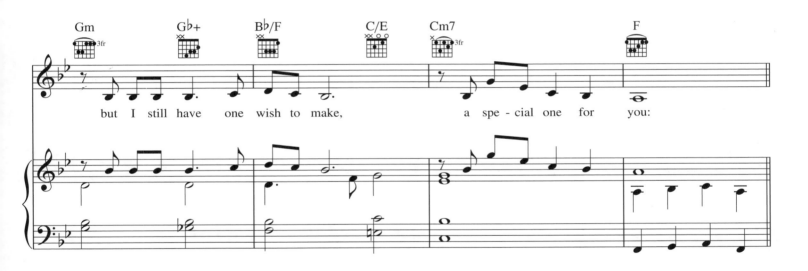

MY FAVORITE THINGS

from THE SOUND OF MUSIC

Lyrics by OSCAR HAMMERSTEIN II
Music by RICHARD RODGERS

NUTTIN' FOR CHRISTMAS

Words and Music by ROY BENNETT
and SID TEPPER

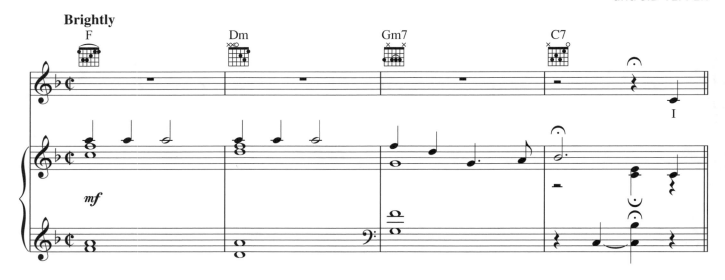

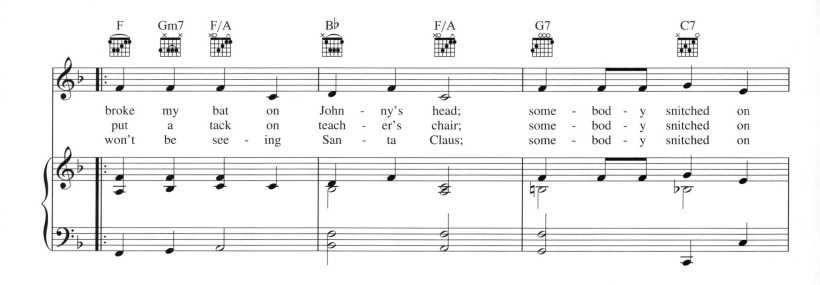

broke my bat on John- ny's head; some- bod- y snitched on
put a tack on teach- er's chair; some- bod- y snitched on
won't be see- ing San- ta Claus; some- bod- y snitched on

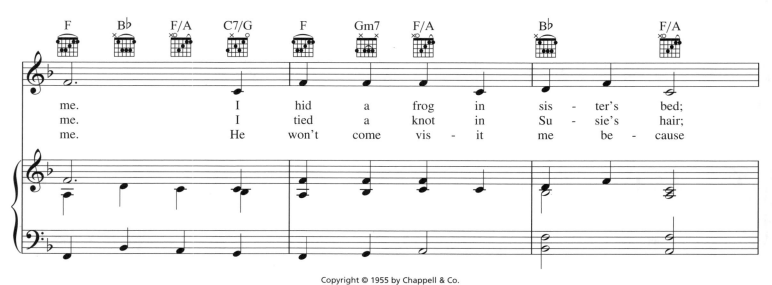

me.   I hid a frog in sis- ter's bed;
me.   I tied a knot in Su- sie's hair;
me.   He won't come vis- it me be- cause

THE NIGHT BEFORE CHRISTMAS SONG

Music by JOHNNY MARKS
Lyrics adapted by JOHNNY MARKS
from CLEMENT MOORE'S Poem

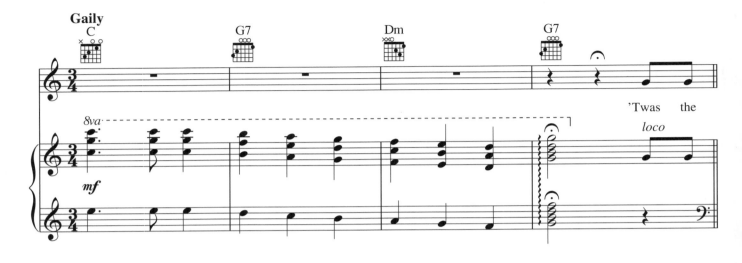

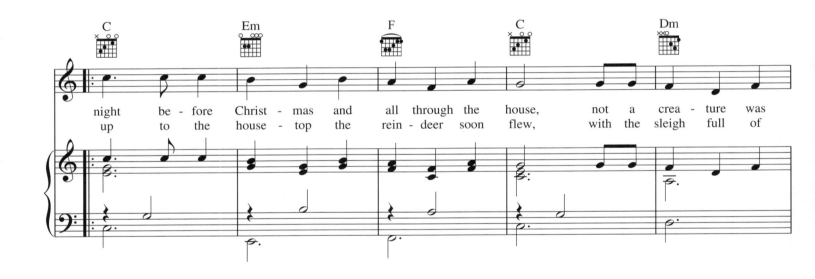

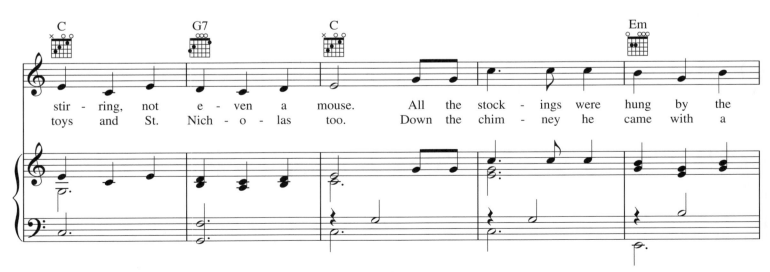

ROCKIN' AROUND THE CHRISTMAS TREE

Music and Lyrics by
JOHNNY MARKS

SANTA, BRING MY BABY BACK
(To Me)

Words and Music by CLAUDE DeMETRUIS
and AARON SCHROEDER

RUDOLPH THE RED-NOSED REINDEER

Music and Lyrics by
JOHNNY MARKS

They nev - er let poor Ru - dolph join in an - y rein - deer

games. Then one fog - gy Christ - mas Eve,

San - ta came to say, "Ru - dolph, with your

nose so bright, won't you guide my sleigh to - night?"

SILVER BELLS

from the Paramount Picture THE LEMON DROP KID

Words and Music by JAY LIVINGSTON
and RAY EVANS

Christ - mas makes you feel e - mo - tion - al. It may bring par - ties or thoughts de - vo - tion - al. What - ev - er hap - pens or what may

THERE IS NO CHRISTMAS LIKE A HOME CHRISTMAS

Written by CARL SIGMAN
and MICKEY ADDY

SILVER AND GOLD

Music and Lyrics by
JOHNNY MARKS

Lyrics:

Sil - ver and gold, sil - ver and gold, ev - 'ry - one wish - es for sil - ver and gold. How do you meas - ure its worth? _____ Just by the pleas - ure it gives here on

THIS IS CHRISTMAS
(Bright, Bright the Holly Berries)

Lyric by WIHLA HUTSON
Music by ALFRED BURT

YOU'RE ALL I WANT FOR CHRISTMAS

Words and Music by GLEN MOORE
and SEGER ELLIS